NSYNC
LARGER THAN LIFE

'N SYNC
LARGER THAN LIFE

★★THE★★
UNOFFICIAL
★BOOK★

SAM HUGHES

BILLBOARD
BOOKS

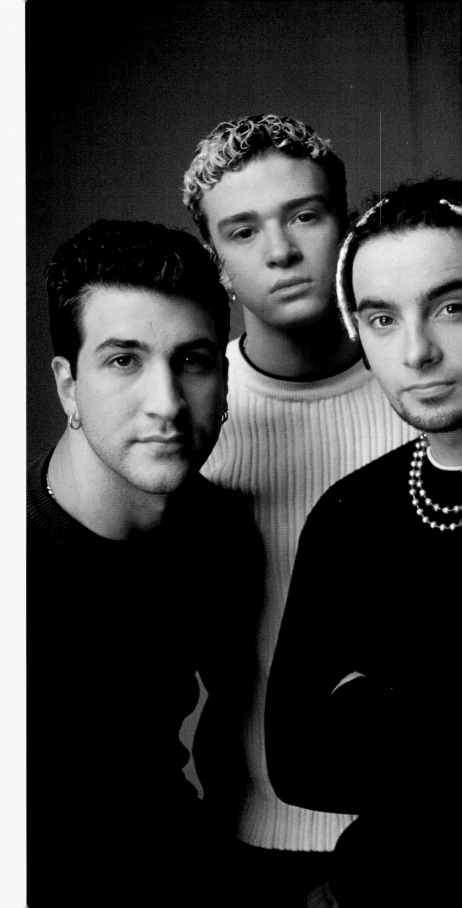

Created in 2001 by
Virgin Books
Thames Wharf Studios
Rainville Road
London
W6 9HA

First published in the United States in
2001 by Billboard Books, an imprint of
Watson-Guptill Publications, a division
of BPI Communications Inc., at
770 Broadway, New York, NY 10003

Library of Congress Cataloging in
Publication data can be obtained
from the Library of Congress.

ISBN 0 8230 8359 4

Printed and bound in Spain
Colour Origination by Colourwise Ltd
Designed by ZiP Design, London
First printing 2001

1 2 3 4 5 6 7 8 9/06 05 04 03 02 01 00

Picture Credits
All Action Doug Peters 32
Alpha 19, 26, 33, 41, 64, 73
Corbis 18, 21, 57
Famous Hubert Boesl 15, 31, 39, 66, 79; Marie
Cristo 36, 48, 54, 67, 77; Mike Kline 65, 71
Retna David Atlas 14, 34; Bob Berg 44; Lillian
Bonomo 59; Larry Busacca 13, 69; Bill Davila
8, 58, 61, 75, 83; Melanie Edwards 17; Steve
Granitz 20, 56; Tim Hale 37; Steve Jennings
82; Bernhard Kuhmstedt 2, 7, 16, 18, 22, 24,
25, 27, 29, 80, 84; Sam Levi 4, 61, 72; Marissa
Roth 50; John Spellman 12, 23, 49, 52; Scott
Weiner 40, 86
South Beach Photo Agency 55; Maggie
Rodriguez 10, 39
Starfile Todd Kaplan 6, 9, 38, 53, 63, 68, 76;
Jeffrey Mayer 46, 62, 70, 74

CONTENTS

★ CHAPTER ONE
THE WORLD AT THEIR FEET

With every phenomenon, whether it is the most talked-about movie, trading card game, pop group or TV show, there is always one defining moment when that phenomenon takes on a life of its own, exploding onto the front pages and making the world sit up and take notice. 'N Sync's moment came on March 21, 2000, with the release of the group's third album, *No Strings Attached*.

The album had been eagerly awaited by 'N Sync's army of devoted fans, who knew what to expect: funky R&B-styled pop, smooth vocal performances and a little of the magic that puts the group head and shoulders above other artists. On the day of release over 7000 fans had gathered in New York's Times Square outside the offices of MTV, hoping to catch a glimpse of Justin, JC, Joey, Lance or Chris. The group's debut self-titled album had reached ten times Platinum status, selling ten million copies around the world and spawning four number one singles, and this had been followed by a highly successful holiday album, *Home for Christmas*. However, the road to *No Strings Attached* had been a rocky one, and though both band and record company knew they had a great album, no one really knew quite how the music would be received by the CD-buying public. They need not have worried. In its

very first week, over 2.4 million copies of *No Strings Attached* were sold in the USA – more than one million of which were on the first day! Instantly the CD became the fastest selling album EVER, beating the record of 1.1 million in one week set by Backstreet Boys the previous year. 'N Sync really was a phenomenon!

Justin, JC, Joey, Lance and Chris were overwhelmed by the incredible reaction from the public, as were their record company, their management and many industry insiders. Mainstream news shows and gossip columnists were quick to run features on the band and their incredible popularity, finally figuring out what teen magazines and their readers had known for some time – these guys were something special!

The album went on to sell over ten million copies, achieving Diamond status and confirming 'N Sync's position as the most popular vocal group in the USA. Even their labelmates the Backstreet Boys, previously considered to have the advantage over 'N Sync in the popularity stakes, failed to match up to 'N Sync's superlative figures when the Boys' fourth CD *Black and Blue* was released in January 2001. The album only sold 1.59 million copies in its first week, leaving the 'N Sync boys clear winners.

Since the release of *No Strings Attached*, 'N Sync have been showered with accolades from all directions. The American Music Awards named them Internet Artist of the Year, reflecting the fact that www.nsync.com was the most visited artist site on the Internet in 2000. In early January the group also picked up the People's Choice Award for Best Musical Group or Band – not surprising considering that *No Strings Attached* was the best-selling album of 2000. Acknowledging the huge number of people behind

The *No Strings Attached* Tour was as superlative as everything connected to 'N Sync in 2000 – over one million tickets were snapped up on the first day they went on sale

'N Sync's success, the group invited their manager, Johnny Wright, and members of their security team on stage with them to collect the award.

'N Sync were also nominated for three 2001 Grammy Awards, and put on a spectacular performance of 'This I Promise You' on the night, with Justin showing off his newly-cropped hairstyle.

'N Sync merchandise is snapped up almost as soon as it hits the stores, and retailers have struggled to keep up with the demand for 'N Sync-related goodies, from T-shirts and mouse-pads to watches and even a board game. The 'N Sync Backstage Pass game pits fans against each other in a trivia test, where correct answers allow the winners to move through an 'N Sync show collecting band members.

In May 2000, 'N Sync started out on an epic 42-date tour to celebrate the remarkable success of their album. The *No Strings Attached* Tour was as superlative as everything connected to 'N Sync in 2000 – over one million tickets were snapped up on the first day they went on sale, and every venue was sold out within hours. Justin called the group's August dates at Madison Square Garden in New York 'the highlight of my career', and the shows attracted a whole bunch of celebrity fans including Rolling Stone Keith Richards, Puff Daddy, Jennifer Lopez and Carson Daly. That same month, Justin, JC, Joey, Lance and Chris also found time to help raise more than half a million dollars by taking part in a charity basketball game for the group's own Challenge for the Children fund.

At the same time as his group was hitting the charts and the record books, Justin also made gossip columns around the world on account of his relationship with another mega-successful young music star, Britney Spears. In MTV interviews backstage after the New York dates, Justin was still denying any romantic involvement with Britney, despite several reported sightings of the pair together. Fans of the cute couple would have to wait until the fall before Justin and Britney finally admitted that they were an item.The holiday season 2000 saw Justin, JC, Joey, Lance and Chris put their 'N Sync-related activities on hold for a few weeks and take some time to recharge their batteries. However, the group did find the time to attend their management company's Christmas party, which was held in a roller-rink in tribute to their manager's previous employment as a roller-skate club manager. Britney Spears joined the group in roller boots, and JC was seen sporting a fetching metallic blue all-in-one jumpsuit.

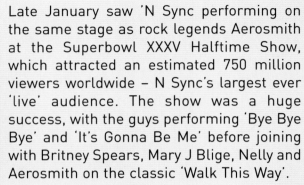

The biggest New Year's Eve party in New York City was hosted by the ever-resourceful Lance

The biggest New Year Eve party in New York City was hosted by the ever-resourceful Lance, who took over the Roseland Ballroom for a $200 a ticket bash which was televised by MTV and ABC. Fans looking out for Britney and Justin together were disappointed however – they kept a low profile, and although some reports stated that they spent New Year's Eve in NYC, others were certain that they'd been spotted at a country club in Denver, Colorado.

Late January saw 'N Sync performing on the same stage as rock legends Aerosmith at the Superbowl XXXV Halftime Show, which attracted an estimated 750 million viewers worldwide – N Sync's largest ever 'live' audience. The show was a huge success, with the guys performing 'Bye Bye Bye' and 'It's Gonna Be Me' before joining with Britney Spears, Mary J Blige, Nelly and Aerosmith on the classic 'Walk This Way'.

In a final blowout live appearance before getting down to work on their new album, 'N Sync flew down to Brazil to headline the huge seven-day Rock in Rio festival, which also featured Britney Spears, Five,

Justin also made gossip columns around the world on account of his relationship with another mega-successful young music star, Britney Spears

Aaron Carter and Brazilian teen act Sandy and Junior. 'N Sync's performance went down a storm in front of 200,000 crazed Brazilian fans, some of whomhad travelled for over 16 hours by bus just to catch a glimpse of their heroes.

So how have the ups and downs of their incredible success during 2000 affected the five very real and very human guys who make up 'N Sync?

JC has revealed that the hardest part of the past year had been the lack of privacy, but that all the guys saw it as a sacrifice that had to be made in order to achieve the career they had always wanted, making the music they love.

In the same interview, Joey talked about another of the pitfalls of fame which the group had encountered: press criticism. Never the darlings of the 'serious' music press, 'N Sync have always tried to ignore critics who brand them 'lightweight and untalented', he said, but he admitted that it's hard to read harsh reviews sometimes: 'It does hurt… that's not your job, that's your life.' Lance added that sometimes the most hurtful thing was to read a review that described a show as 'great… if you like that sort of thing.'

Watching the group's appearance on the *Larry King Live* TV show in January 2001, it was clear that every member of the group had become more confident and laid back

in front of an audience, and had learnt how to field difficult questions with charm and wit. During the interview, Chris revealed that another reason the guys felt assured enough to goof around on stage was that they all started out as friends, and made it clear that there was still a real chemistry between the five best buddies.

King remarked that the boys seemed a little more grown-up, less energetic and calmer than the

'N Sync's performance went down a storm in front of 200,000 crazed Brazilian fans

bundles of energy that first burst onto the music scene in 1998. Lance agreed, reasoning that the group's gruelling tour schedule and endless interviews left them with less energy all round. All the group were quick to counter suggestions that they were suffering a lack of enthusiasm, however, and as if to prove it they announced a 35-date summer stadium tour to promote their forthcoming album. On the tour they promised to take their funky pop to a whole new level.

'N Sync has produced some of the most power-ful, energetic and heartfelt music around today. In the future they will continue to push musical boundaries and to respect to the people who matter most: their fans. Those fans are right to be proud of Justin, JC, Joey, Lance and Chris – five guys who have given their all to become five of America's most sought-after and successful young men.

★ CHAPTER TWO
JUSTIN UP CLOSE

Ask any group of 'N Sync fans their number one heartthrob, and you can guarantee the answer – Justin Timberlake. Justin has inspired the creation of countless websites, his face appears on millions of posters on bedroom walls around the world, and he is the subject of more gossip and media interest than all the other band members put together. Maybe it's his cute curly hair, his stunning looks or his energetic, magnetic personality – or maybe it's his relationship with a certain Ms Spears – but whatever makes people so interested in Justin, you can be sure that he won't let the attention change his sweet nature.

Justin was born on January 31, 1981 to Lynn and Randy Timberlake, in Memphis, Tennessee, a city with a strong musical heritage. Lynn and Randy split up when Justin was just a toddler, although Justin still sees Randy and his new wife Lisa regularly. Lynn later married Paul Harless, and Justin now has two younger half-brothers, Jonathan, seven, and Steven, who's just two years old, and according to Justin can already do a passable 'human beatbox' impression! Justin is very close to his whole family, especially his mother and stepfather, and he has said that the worst part of being on the road with 'N Sync is the fact that he doesn't get the chance to see Jonathan and Steven growing up.

Justin showed his natural musical talent at a remarkably young age, singing harmonies along with the car radio before he could read or write. From the age of eight he took voice lessons and was soon singing in the church choir and performing solos during services, an experience which would prove inspiring to the talented youngster in the years ahead.

The young Justin loved to perform outside the church environment too, both in school musicals and at talent shows, which he regularly won. Once he and a

group of friends dressed up as the teen idols of the time, New Kids On The Block, and performed their hit 'Please Don't Go Girl' to an admiring school assembly. The show was such a hit that they were invited to travel to a nearby school to repeat the performance – by hired limo, of course – and were chased down the corridors by groups of adoring girls.

After this first taste of fame, Justin was hooked! He took part in more talent shows in the local area, and his mother Lynn even drove him to Orlando, Florida to take part in the nationally-syndicated TV show *Star Search*. Unfortunately, despite a confident performance Justin came second, beaten by a little girl who performed a show tune from a Broadway musical. Who knows, maybe she's an 'N Sync fan now?

While Justin and Lynn waited around backstage at *Star Search*, Justin was intrigued to discover that the *Mickey Mouse Club* TV show was recorded on a nearby sound stage. This long-running Disney show, which had recently been revived for the 1990s, was a particular fave of Justin's, and for some time he had

dreamed of appearing as one of the show's Mouseketeers. He heard that the show was holding open auditions for the next season in various cities around the country, and persuaded his mother to drive him the few hundred miles to Nashville, Tennessee to try out for it. At the auditions, the twelve-year old Justin sang and danced his heart out, and eventually triumphed over 30,000 kids from across the country who had auditioned for one of the seven places on offer. He was in the club!

During his two years on the show, Justin sang, danced and performed comedy sketches, in many cases paired with his buddy JC Chasez. He also became great friends with the other Mouseketeers, many of whom would go on to greater things – stars like Christina Aguilera, Keri Russell and of course Britney Spears, a cute Louisiana girl with whom Justin kept in touch over the next few years.

Justin's experience as a young presenter of the *Mickey Mouse Club* TV show taught him at an early age how the showbiz industry works, and he has been careful to differentiate between long-term friends and temporary hangers-on who just want to

During downtime, maybe hanging out backstage or chilling in a hotel room, Justin loves to surf the net just like the rest of us. Unsurprisingly he can often be found checking out basketball and entertainment sites, although he admits that he has a short attention span and gets impatient if he can't find what he's looking for online straight away. While driving he likes to listen to a wide range of different music, from Bryan McKnight to Eminem, an artist he admires even though the controversial rapper has proclaimed his hatred of 'N Sync. Justin also likes to check out the radio, but he has admitted that he hears his own songs so often that if a radio station starts playing an 'N Sync track he'll change the channel!

When he really kicks back and enjoys a nap on the tour bus or plane, the other members of the band listen in, because Justin has a reputation for talking in his sleep. Although he's not revealed any embarrassing secrets yet, the guys might find some fascinating stuff if they just keep their ears open...!

The other guys in the band joke with Justin about the attention he gets from the media and the fans, and during photoshoots they have been known to quietly sing 'Don't Speak' by No Doubt, a reference to the media's habit of focusing on that band's beautiful singer Gwen Stefani while sidelining the other guys.

While JC, Joey, Lance and Chris get their fair share of attention, it's a fact of life that for many, many 'N Sync fans, it's Justin who gets top marks for cuteness every time.

During 'N Sync's debut headlining tour of the USA in the winter of 1998, Justin was lucky enough to hook up with an old friend from *MMC*, a girl who had recently experienced a phenomenal debut with

a song called '...Baby One More Time'. Britney Spears was one of the opening acts for 'N Sync's shows at the time, but she soon became one of the biggest female stars today. After this chance reunion Britney and Justin became even closer than they had been at *MMC*, not least because they had both been flung into the spotlight at a very young age, and as a result had similar experiences to bond them together.

Britney and Justin were first romantically linked soon after this tour, and gossip abounded about the pair's secret meetings in New York and Memphis, and the presents they were said to have bought each other – some gossip columnists even alleged that Justin and Britney were living together. Although some of Justin's admirers found it hard to accept that he might not be single, the majority of 'N Sync's fans gave the relationship their blessing long before the pair made their love public.

know him because he's famous. No matter who he hangs out with when on tour with 'N Sync, he can be sure that he will always be surrounded by four firm friends who'll stick together forever – JC, Joey, Lance and Chris.

The youngest member of 'N Sync by almost two years, Justin has always been the most confident

Ever since 'N Sync first came to the attention of the media, interviewers have marvelled at Justin's natural charm and easy going nature – unusual in someone who did his growing up in front of the camera from the age of twelve. Everyone who has met Justin remarks on his genuine lack of pretensions, despite the fact that he is one of the most desirable and sought-after men in the world, with millions of adoring female fans. This guy's just too modest!

That's not to say Justin doesn't have his faults. He admits to being terribly grumpy in the mornings – at least until he gets a bowl of cereal to kick-start his system. He can't sit still either, and can often be found in the gym working out, an activity which he says allows him to relax and focus his mind.

Though he's the youngest member of 'N Sync by almost two years, Justin has always been the most confident of the five, both on and off stage. Never afraid to speak up when band matters are being discussed, Justin has always known what he wants for the group, and makes it clear that he's learned lot about the business side of music since the band started.

Justin has been a crazed basketball fan from an early age, and when he's not on stage or resting you can be sure to find him shooting a few hoops with his buddies. His first sporting hero was Michael Jordan, which led him to lend his support to the North Carolina Tarheels, and in many early photos of 'N Sync you can see him sporting the team's trademark light blue jersey. He also follows the Chicago Bulls, and expresses an admiration for his adopted hometown team, the Orlando Magic. In the rare occasions that he can get on the B-ball court for a game, Justin admits that he's a pretty good defensive player, and claims that passing is one of his specialities because he used to play at point guard.

In August 2000, Britney and Justin were spotted dancing intimately in a Manhattan nightclub, although when questioned Justin laughed at suggestions that they were engaged. Later in the year it became harder for the pair to disguise their love. It was Britney who first admitted the truth in a series of interviews with teen magazines in the winter of 2000, revealing that the couple had been an item for two years, and that they were both very much in love. Justin has since come clean about his feelings for Britney, calling her a wonderful person who is his 'reality check' in the unreal world of pop megastardom.

Since the relationship became public knowledge, the couple have relaxed the secrecy surrounding their personal lives, and fans have been able to see just how well-matched and happy Britney and Justin are together. On Britney's 19th birthday, she appeared on stage with 'N Sync at a show in San Diego, California, disguised in a wig and sunglasses. When Britney took these off she received a large cheer, before Justin encouraged the crowd to sing her 'Happy Birthday'. For Christmas 2000 Britney is said to have given

Justin a $30,000 Patek Philippe watch, engraved with the words:' To my Justin, love you always, Britney'.

In early 2001, fans of funky pop music went wild when MTV's Carson Daly announced that 'N Sync and Britney would be performing live together in a massive summer tour. Disappointingly for fans of both acts, Jive Records soon got in touch with the studio to deny the story, but you can be sure that the pair will find ways to be near each other as much as possible during the coming year. Justin has also hinted that, if there was enough interest, he would consider recording a duet with his girlfriend. Watch this space...!

So what's next for Justin and Britney? At the time of writing the couple are not officially engaged, although she has said that they would like to get married once they are both 21 and feel ready to make that commitment. For now, both Britney and Justin are happy to support each other through the highs and lows of life in the public eye. No doubt 'N Sync's fans will wish this beautiful and successful couple well, no matter what the future holds.

JUSTIN FACTS

★ Justin's most recent nickname is Butter; others include Bounce and The Baby

★ Justin's worst habit is belching loudly

★ When he was at school Justin had a reputation for being able to talk himself out of trouble with the teachers, no matter what he did!

★ Justin has dyed his hair almost every color of the rainbow, including red, blonde, green and baby blue

★ His fave cartoon character is Bugs Bunny

★ Lance's fave TV show of all time is *I Love Lucy*, and his number one actress is Lucille Ball

★ Justin has launched a charitable foundation to raise money for music and arts in public schools

★ Justin has said that he never tires of performing because the fans make each show different

★ Justin's fave 'N Sync track is '(God Must Have Spent) A Little More Time on You'

★ For Christmas 2000, Justin's gift to himself was a huge aquarium full of tropical fish

★ Justin's heroes are Stevie Wonder and Michael Jordan

★ He admits to being a shopaholic, with a taste for smart designer wear

★ Justin's first kiss was in sixth grade, with a girl called Mindy

CHAPTER THREE

THE ROAD TO SUCCESS

So how did five young guys from far-flung parts of the USA get together to form the world-beating musical sensation that is 'N Sync? Surely such a perfect combination of talented, good-looking guys couldn't have bumped into each other just by chance?

Unlike many successful pop groups, the members of 'N Sync were not recruited from hundreds of hope-fuls and introduced only in the rehearsal room. All five members of the group were friends, harmonizing and rehearsing their moves in their spare time, long before they had a record company or even professional management.

The 'N Sync story starts way back in 1993, when the twelve-year old Justin Timberlake moved with his family to Orlando, Florida to appear on the *Mickey Mouse Club* TV show. Justin and his new pal JC quickly bonded over basketball and their love of singing, becoming firm friends both on and off set.

When the *Mickey Mouse Club* was cancelled in October 1994, Justin returned to Memphis, but his heart had

been captured by the thrill of performing in front of an audience. He soon became bored with high school life, and looked for a way to work in the music industry, either on stage or behind the scenes. Getting nowhere in his attempts to start a solo singing career, and realizing that two heads are often better than one, Justin called up his old friend JC, who jumped at the chance to visit Memphis and record some demo songs with Justin. The two firmly believed that they had the talent to make it big one way or another, but they realized that they both needed to be based closer to the home of an established entertainment industry: Orlando, Florida.

In another brave and decisive step that turned out to be a blessing, Justin and his mother, Lynn, moved to Orlando to join his friend, with Lynn acting as manager and mentor to the pair and arranging vocal training, rehearsals and demo recordings.

Meanwhile, New York-born Joey Fatone was gaining useful entertainment experience appearing in monster make-up in the Beetlejuice Graveyard Revue at Universal Studios, Florida. There he met

Justin with his mother, Lynn.

Chris Kirkpatrick, a talented singer who was marking time waiting for his big break by performing with a doo-wop group, the Hollywood Hightones. Sharing an interest in pretty girls and an ambition to break into the mainstream music industry, Joey and Chris hit it off from day one, and spent hours plotting how to fulfill their dreams of musical fame. Joey was friends with JC through some high-school friends who also performed on *MMC*, so when Chris realized that his best chance of stellar musical success was as part of a vocal group, Chris and Joey joined Justin and JC in the fledgling group.

In August 1995 the five-piece was complete. Or almost. At the time, the bass harmonies were performed by another friend from the Orlando performing community, who eventually proved unable to commit enough of his spare time to rehearsals and had to leave the group. The four guys' harmonies and dance routines were improving continuously, but despite Joey's attempts to fill the vacant bass part, there was still an element missing from the group's sound. The band members asked around on the Orlando music scene for a recommendation – a cool, dependable guy with a soulful bass voice. Luckily, JC's old vocal coach knew of an aptly named youngster, Lance Bass, who at the time was a diligent high school student with an ambition to join NASA.

Chris immediately realized that 'N Sync would be a pretty cool name for their group

Justin called up Lance, who despite being a keen amateur singer had no burning desire to make it big in the entertainment industry. There was also the obstacle of Lance's mother. All the guys were convinced that she wouldn't allow her son to leave school and join a pop group. However, after speaking to Justin for a very short time, Lance was convinced that this opportunity was too good to miss. He persuaded his mom, and the very next day Lance flew to Orlando to perform 'The Star Spangled Banner' with the other four guys. As soon as they heard the result, Justin, JC, Joey and Chris were overjoyed – they had found their fifth and final member.

Still without a management deal or record company interest, the group held down day jobs and rehearsed at odd hours of the night, perfecting their dance routines in an old warehouse with no air-conditioning down the street from Justin's mother's house. Lynn was often present at these rehearsals, providing soft drinks and encouragement whenever the guys took a break. After one particularly impressive vocal performance, she happened to remark that the five guys sounded particularly in sync. Chris immediately realized that 'N Sync would be a pretty cool name for their group, not just because it accurately described their effortless vocal prowess, but also because 'N Sync was also an almost-perfect acronym formed from the last letters of each of their names: JustiN, ChriS, JoeY and JC. Not put off by the fact that the newest member of the group's name didn't quite fit, they nicknamed him LansteN for the sake of completeness. What a cool way to get your nickname!

In October 1995 the hard work of rehearsals had paid off, and 'N Sync were ready to take their show to the world. With a bit of help from their friends on the Orlando entertainment scene, the group arranged a special gig to showcase their talents at Walt Disney World's Pleasure Island nightclub. Dressed in matching clothing and with a bunch of familiar faces cheering them on, the boys performed a fifteen minute show featuring choreographed dance moves performed to a pre-recorded backing track of covers, including a funked-up version of the Beatles' 'We Can Work It Out'. The entire show was captured on video by a friend of Justin and JC who had been a cameraman on the *Mickey Mouse Club* and wanted to help out his old co-workers on the next step to stardom.

Although the guys admit to being a little embarrassed by the inevitable rough edges in their performance, the tape was good enough for them to send out as a promo video to a number of record companies and industry contacts. In early 1996, the tape found its way to Louis J. Pearlman, who at the time was business manager of the Backstreet Boys. Pearlman was impressed with what he saw, and sent the tape to his right-hand man, Johnny Wright, who was working with the Backstreet Boys in Germany at the time.

The group had certainly heard of Wright – he managed the day-to-day affairs of the Backstreet Boys, and had been road manager for one of the most successful male vocal groups ever, New Kids On The Block. All of the members of 'N Sync had idolized the New Kids while growing up, and knew that Wright and Pearlman were the ones who had made it happen for that group. Now this guy was flying in from Europe to meet them!

Although he was the driving force behind the phenomenal success of the Backstreet Boys, a group with a comparable sound and appeal to that of 'N Sync, as soon as Wright met the band he had no reservations about taking on another five-piece group based in Florida. He reasoned that the guys were just too talented to ignore, and that by bringing 'N Sync to a wider audience he could give fans of vocal groups more variety and more great music. He quickly signed up the boys, put them in touch with professional choreographers and recording studios, and created slick demo tapes and videos which would help the group get record deals around the world. 'N Sync were finally on their way!

You might think that the instantly recognisable, hi-tech and super-catchy sound that characterizes artists such as Backstreet Boys and Britney Spears would be created in some huge studio complex in the sunny southern states of the USA. However, these artists and many others have recorded their biggest hits on the other side of the Atlantic Ocean, in a small studio called Cheiron on the outskirts of chilly Stockholm, Sweden. And it was to Cheiron that 'N Sync headed in late 1996, accompanied by Johnny Wright, to work with Max Martin, who would later write '...Baby One More Time', and the late Denniz Pop, who had produced hits for Five, Ace of Base and the Backstreet Boys. Recording with these and other European producers including Full Force, 'N Sync soon had a bunch of new R&B-charged pop songs with which to mount their assault on the worldwide pop charts.

Following the same route that Backstreet Boys had taken the previous year, in 1997 'N Sync resolved to make it big in Europe before tackling the rock-dominated charts of their home country. Both 'Tearin' Up My Heart' and 'I Want You Back' were released on the BMG Ariola Munich record label in Germany and Sweden, the former hitting the shops just 28 days after the group had signed their recording deal. As the guys toured Europe to promote the songs, winning over audiences and gaining a huge following, both singles became platinum-selling hits.

BMG soon released 'N Sync's self-titled debut album, which followed the singles to the highest reaches of the charts right across Europe. It took a while for 'N Sync to adjust to their new found fame, and more than one member has remarked on the odd sensation of being mobbed in a foreign country while remaining totally unknown in one's home town.

In the spring of 1998, 'I Want You Back' was released in the USA, a signal for the band to return to Florida to a nightmare schedule of personal appearances at radio stations, county fairs and shopping malls, not to mention countless support slots with established acts. The single was a slow starter but eventually became an enormous hit, remaining in the *Billboard* charts for over six months and peaking at number thirteen. It received a massive amount of airplay across the country, as radio listeners responded to its catchy vibe and heavy beat. Fans were desperate for more information about these cute guys, and teen magazines were keen to snag them as cover stars.

Making sure to catch the wave of enthusiasm that they could sense building, 'N Sync released the US version of their debut self-titled album, which featured new tracks recorded in Orlando as well as the best of the European album, at the end of March. The album didn't take off immediately, but the band took every opportunity to take their songs to the audience they knew was out there. In July 1998, they struck lucky. Backstreet Boys had been forced to pull out of a planned *In Concert* special for the Disney Channel, so 'N Sync stepped into their shoes and were clearly overjoyed to be filmed performing and in interviews at the Disney-MGM Studios. Suddenly, within weeks of the concert being aired on July 18, 1998, sales of *'N Sync* began to pick up, catapulting it into the *Billboard* Top Ten, where it would remain for several months. 'N Sync had arrived!

CHAPTER FOUR

JC UP CLOSE

Joshua Scott Chasez, or JC as he is known to all but his parents, is without doubt the most serious member of 'N Sync, the guy who's most focused on songwriting and getting the band's music just right. But don't imagine that he isn't fascinating company: this sensitive guy comes across as deeply sincere and thoughtful, always taking time to choose his words carefully before answering a question.

Professional to a fault, JC often takes on the role of spokesman for the rest of the band, and is usually the one chosen to communicate the message the group is trying to put across in press conferences. JC's

JC's piercing blue eyes and sculpted cheekbones have also made him a favorite with female fans

piercing blue eyes and sculpted cheekbones have also made him a favorite with female fans, a situation he handles with gentlemanly charm and self-effacing modesty.

JC certainly doesn't have a proud or vain bone in his body, and has always said he prefers the band's music to be judged on its own merits rather than on the personalities of the five. He is quick to admit his

faults too, revealing that he always puts off things that he has to do until tomorrow, and that he can be lazy and grouchy when he hasn't had enough sleep.

In fact, JC has gained quite a reputation as the sleepy-head of the group: whenever they get on the tour bus after the show, you can bet that it's JC who'll be fast asleep before any of the others. He has said that if he was a Spice Girl he'd be Sleepy Spice (or Serious Spice), and that he makes use of the stuffed toys fans give to him by substituting them for pillows on the tour bus!

Born in Washington D.C. on August 8, 1976, little Josh could certainly claim to come from a well-connected family – his father networked computers at the White House! When JC was just a baby, his mother Karen and father Roy moved out to the suburb of Bowie, Maryland, a comfortable area and a safe environment to bring up a young family. Soon the little guy was joined by a sister, Heather, and a baby brother, Tyler.

Apart from listening to the radio, the Chasez household wasn't particularly musical, except at Christmas, when the family would sing carols around the tree. Although he knew he was a fairly good singer, as he grew up JC was much more interested

in sports like football and basketball, and thought he might like to take up a practical career when he was older, working on antique cars or making furniture.

At the age of twelve, JC was doing what most kids do, hanging out at friends' houses and going to youth clubs to meet girls. He had also gained quite a reputation as a dancer, attending classes to improve his technique, but the hobby wasn't really a big thing for him. Some of the girls he knew were planning to perform at an upcoming talent show, and asked shy JC to join them in their dance routine. His friend KC urged him to participate, and the two joined in with the routine, which was set to MC Hammer's hit 'Can't Touch This'. To everyone's surprise, the schoolfriends won the competition, and this led to more talent show victories for the group in the local area.

It was JC's mother, Karen, who first heard of the auditions for the *Mickey Mouse Club* taking place in Washington D.C. when JC was just thirteen. JC really didn't think he had a chance; after all, he was going for one of ten positions against a total of 20,000 kids from right across the country. Nevertheless, he did his best at the open audition, and ended up being selected to appear on the show.

JC has said that getting his place on *MMC* was one of the greatest moments of his life: not only did it pave the way for his future career with 'N Sync, but it introduced him to a group of friends with whom he knows he will stay in touch for life. One of JC's closest friends during his time at *MMC* was Keri Russell, now famous as TV's *Felicity*; and in his final year on the show JC was to become best friends with another talented youngster, Justin Timberlake.

The teenage JC spent most of his time on the show performing in comedy sketches and dance routines, and like any professional he continued to attend dance classes to hone his skills. JC was also a talented if self-conscious singer, with the rare gift of perfect pitch, so his dance teacher was pleased when he expressed an interest in entering a singing talent competition. She paid for his entry without actually having heard him sing, and was proud to see her student take first prize with an assured performance of the Richard Marx hit 'Right Here Waiting for You'. It was the realization that his musical talents were something special that encouraged JC to work with his friend Justin on building a pop career, an ambition that would soon lead to the birth of 'N Sync.

Talented JC puts a great deal of effort into his songwriting; four of the tracks on *No Strings Attached* are credited to him

After the band's number one heartthrob, Justin, it's JC who receives the largest amount of fan mail from female admirers. But what does he look for in a girlfriend, and is he single at the moment? JC has always said that his ideal woman would need to be extremely patient and understanding to cope with his crazy schedule and the long hours he loves to spend working. It looks like JC might have found just the right girl in Bobbee, a model and journalist who appeared in the 'I Drive Myself Crazy' video, and who also works for *J-14* magazine. JC and Bobbee have been seen together at premières and award shows, and although JC has played down the seriousness of the relationship, things are looking good for this well-matched couple.

Strangely for someone who discovered his love of singing relatively late in his performing career, JC's whole life now revolves around music. He is happiest sitting down at a keyboard, working out a melody line or composing some lyrics, and whenever he can grab some spare time out of the band's commitments you'll find him in the studio, writing songs or remixing tracks for 'N Sync or for other artists.

When it comes to musical inspiration, JC idolizes artists who have combined classic songwriting with commercial success. He admires Sting hugely, citing 'Fragile' as one of his favorite songs ever, and is also inspired by Seal, Brian McKnight and Boyz II Men. Out of 'N Sync's own songs, JC would have to choose 'For The Girl Who Has Everything' as his fave; he has said that he loves the way it builds up to an emotional peak.

A true perfectionist, JC is modest about his songwriting; he reckons that 'not everything I've written is great – I'm still learning.' For a

beginner, he's done pretty well so far. As well as writing and performing on a track for Boyz'n'Girls United, JC has also written several tracks for the girl band Wild Orchid. JC has a special bond with this group: he has been close friends with Stacy Ferguson and Renee Sandstrom, two-thirds of Wild Orchid, since they appeared on *Kids, Inc.*, a TV show which was made at the same time as JC was appearing on the *Mickey Mouse Club*. JC has recalled his inspiration for writing one of Wild Orchid's songs came from a weekend in Las Vegas playing cards with the girls. Stacy was on a winning streak, and started calling herself 'Fireball Ferguson'. JC remembered this nickname, and later came up with the song 'I'm On Fire'.

Talented JC puts a great deal of effort into his songwriting; four of the tracks on *No Strings Attached* are credited to him, and he would love 'N Sync to record many more of his songs in the future. Always striving for perfection in 'N Sync's stage performances, he has said that it 'means so much more when you're singing your own songs'. He has also revealed that what he really loves about songwriting is the satisfaction of reaching out to people; one day he'd love to come up with a classic which will be remembered for years to come and be recorded by other artists. It's a farsighted and admirable ambition for a young musician, and judging by the success he's achieved so far, we can look forward to hearing lots more from this naturally gifted and hard-working guy in the future.

JC FACTS

★ JC isn't impressed by designer labels – he'd rather wear a comfy pair of jeans and a pair of boots any day

★ JC loves Chinese food

★ His fave Jelly Belly beans are cotton candy, pear and root beer

★ Justin has dyed his hair almost every color of the rainbow, including red, blond, green and baby blue

★ JC's first celebrity crush was on Janet Jackson

★ If he could swap places with anyone for a day, he'd like to be a woman just to see what it was like to experience the world from a female perspective

★ JC supports his hometown football team, the Washington Redskins

★ JC collects Hard Rock Café menus from around the world, and has more than 30 lining the walls of his bedroom at his parents' house

★ His party trick is to do handsprings!

★ JC claims that the best thing about being famous is getting free ice-cream at McDonalds!

★ He is the group's biggest romantic, and once serenaded a girl with a song he had written specially for the occasion

★ JC's first kiss was a scary experience: he was pinned down by four girls in a game of tag, while another girl kissed him

★ The ideal evening for JC would be a quiet night in with a pizza and a movie

★ JC has been linked romantically with members of three separate girl groups: Lindsay from B*Witched, Nikki from Innosense and Stacy from Wild Orchid

★ CHAPTER FIVE
TEARIN' UP THE CHARTS

When 'N Sync released their second US single, 'Tearin' Up My Heart', in the summer of 1998, things really began to take off for them in a big way. The single stormed the *Billboard* charts, peaking at number five, and by September 1998 their debut album had gone double Platinum in the US and Canada, a phenomenal achievement when you consider that the band had been completely unknown

in their own country less than a year before. Things were moving fast for the guys, and the following two years would pass in a blur. They were prepared to work hard, however: when he first met the band, Johnny Wright had impressed on them the

importance of taking every opportunity to make their band a long-term success while they were hot. There would be no time for vacations or weekends off for these guys!

On October 14, 1998, 'N Sync set off on their first large-scale concert dates, supporting Janet Jackson on her *Velvet Rope* tour. It was a dream come true for the guys, who had grown up listening to the singer's hits, including 'Control' and 'Rhythm Nation', and Chris has recalled that he was blown away by Janet's modesty and talent.

For the 1998 winter holiday season, Justin, JC, Lance, Chris and Joey wanted to give their new fans something special, so 'N Sync headed into the studio to record *Home for Christmas*, a seasonal combination of classic holiday songs and new romantic tunes written specially for the group.

The recording of the album had to be squeezed into just fourteen days in order to meet the CD's tight production schedule in time for the holiday season. Backing tracks had been laid down in advance by producers working in their own studios across America, and the band were already familiar with old standards such as 'The First Noel' and 'The

Christmas Song (Chestnuts Roasting On An Open Fire)', a song made famous by Nat King Cole. In the studio, the guys were able to focus solely on the harmonies and vocal arrangements, giving the whole album a mellow R&B feel that would be the blueprint for some of the slower-paced songs on their next album.

While *Home for Christmas* was being rushed into stores across America for its release date of November 10, Justin, Joey, Lance, Chris and JC were gearing up for their first-ever headlining dates in the USA. This was the first time that many fans had been given the opportunity to see their fave group's spectacular dance routines at close range, and they were absolutely blown away by the sheer energy of the 'N Sync live experience. The group have always made it clear that playing live is very important to them – after all, it's their chance to give something back in person to all those fans who have put them at the top of the charts.

The tour kicked off on November 18, 1998, fittingly in the band's hometown of Orlando, Florida. 'N Sync's first major headlining tour was a monster, spanning almost six months and taking in almost every sizeable city on the continent of North America. Opening acts on the tour's various legs included teen R&B star Tatyana Ali , Irish girl group B*witched, girl band Wild Orchid and another ex-Mouseketeer, Britney Spears.

Despite a gruelling schedule in which almost every night was spent fitfully trying to catch a few hours' sleep on a tour bus, the guys found time to make a number of TV appearances, particularly during the Christmas period. They were glad to be invited back for their second appearance on *Live! With Regis and Kathie Lee*, and this was followed up by slots on *CBS This Morning, the Ricki Lake Show* and *Walt Disney World's Very Merry Christmas* Parade on ABC.

Although it was still relatively early in the band's career, the guys were already beginning to pick up awards. When 'N Sync received their first Platinum album in September 1998, all the guys (except JC) celebrated by getting 'N Sync tattoos. At the American Music Awards, 'N Sync won Best New Artist, and at the *Billboard* Music Video awards in December 1998 the band walked away with the awards for Best Dance Clip and Best Dance New Artist Clip for 'I Want You Back'.

'N Sync's New Year's Eve celebrations included a sold-out Las Vegas concert, and their new year was made even better by the release to radio of every 'N Sync fan's fave romantic track, '(God Must Have Spent) A Little More Time On You'. Although this was never available as a single in stores, it reached number 34 on the *Billboard* Hot 100 on airplay alone, and found a place in the hearts of music fans everywhere with its heartfelt and sincere message.

As the tour drew to a close in April 1999, the guys triumphantly returned home to Orlando for a sold-out five-night stint. Their joy as they greeted the local fans who had supported them since their early days was tempered by

concern for their colleague Lance, who had been confined to hospital a few days previously, reportedly suffering from exhaustion. Lance later confirmed that he had been hospitalized due to a minor heart condition, and expressed regret at not being able to join the other guys on stage. The majority of *No Strings Attached* was recorded in the early summer

of 1999, as the guys took a break from touring and looked to the future. However, storm clouds were on the horizon, and legal problems with their record company meant that the album would not meet its planned November 1999 release date.

Unwilling to let behind-the-scenes wrangling get in the way of making great music, 'N Sync threw themselves into collaborations with other artists, gaining respect from the musical community and introducing new fans to their music. The group had already collaborated with Phil Collins on the soundtrack to Disney's Tarzan, an experience which left 'N Sync starstruck and Collins awed at the talent and professionalism of his new young friends. The band also joined forces with Gloria Estefan to record the Oscar-nominated song 'Music Of My Heart', the theme to the movie of the same name, which was also nominated for Best Pop Collaboration at the 42nd Annual Grammy Awards.

Perhaps the group's most surprising and critically acclaimed collaboration was with country legends Alabama, who had approached 'N Sync's management to request permission to record '(God Must

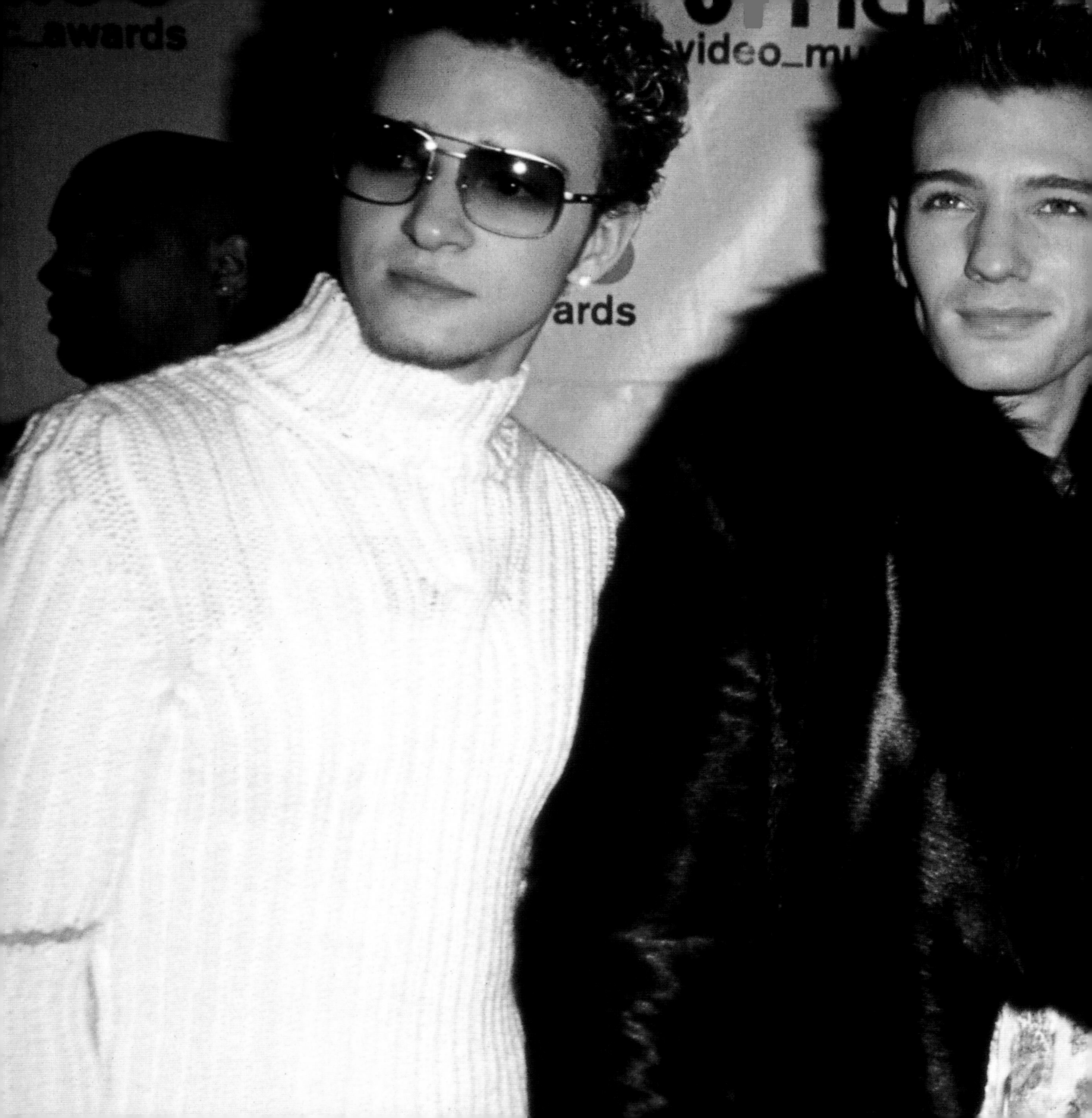
awards

Back in 1998, 'N Sync's debut album and singles had been released by RCA Records, and the boys' development as a band had been bankrolled by Lou Pearlman, the business brain behind Backstreet Boys and head of Trans Continental Records. Now that the 'N Sync boys had tasted success and had learned more about the record industry, they began to feel they weren't getting the best deal from RCA and Trans Continental, both financially and in terms of creative freedom. In a surprise move that was the talk of the music world, 'N Sync's manager Johnny Wright announced that 'N Sync was leaving RCA and signing with Jive Records, home of Britney Spears

Soon RCA's parent company, BMG Music, launched a $150 million lawsuit against 'N Sync and Jive

and Backstreet Boys. Not only did this cause serious problems with 'N Sync's old record company, but there were also suggestions of a conflict of interest at Jive – after all, they already had Backstreet Boys, so why sign another act with a similar audience?

Soon RCA's parent company, BMG Music, launched a $150 million lawsuit against 'N Sync and Jive, accusing 'N Sync of turning their backs on Pearlman and RCA now that they were famous, and trying to prevent 'N Sync from recording, performing or even existing ever again. 'N Sync then launched a $25 million counterclaim against their old record company and Trans Continental, alleging that they had been exploited and swindled by Pearlman and that he had taken a disproportionate proportion of their earnings for himself. Lawyers' statements bounced back and forth, monitored eagerly by the

group's young fans, many of whom were fascinated by the legal battle that threatened the career of their fave band.

On the day before Thanksgiving 1999, Judge Anne Conway heard the arguments of both sides. The Trans Continental team tried to convince her that the group should not be allowed to move to Jive until at least 2002, but the judge threw out this request. Instead, she ruled that the band could join Jive once an out-of-court settlement had been reached with BMG and Pearlman. The two sides sat down and thrashed out a deal, the details of which remain secret to this day. However, the outcome in early 2000 meant that 'N Sync were able to build on the support BMG had given them in the past, while forging a new relationship with Jive.

After the stress of the previous six months, in which others had tried to control every aspect of the band's career and even tried to prevent them using their name, Justin, JC, Joey, Lance and Chris were determined to prove that they were no puppets. After a triumphant debut performance of their new single, 'Bye Bye Bye', at the American Music Awards, 'N Sync prepared to release their long awaited and much delayed third album, *No Strings Attached*, on March 21, 2000.

It would be a week that they would remember for the rest of their lives.

★ CHAPTER SIX
CHRIS UP CLOSE

You might think that the oldest member of 'N Sync, the one who got the band together in the early days, would be the most mature and sensible of the five today. Well you'd be wrong – very wrong! Chris Kirkpatrick has always had a crazy streak, and even as he approaches his thirtieth birthday he retains his off-the-wall wit and spontaneous energy. As unprepared interviewers have found to their cost, he is always ready with a funny quip or a deadpan response, no matter how straightforward or sincere the question. In online chats you can be sure he'll be the one who comes up with a nonsensical or over-the-top answer for every question posted.

Chris would be the first to admit that he has a very short attention span – nothing can keep him occupied for long, and he changes his hairstyle like he changes his mind. Since the band started, Chris's hair has gone from black to brown to blue, and from short to curly to braided. What he will come up with next is anyone's guess!

Although he might occasionally come across as flippant, the truth is that Chris only makes funny comments to make others laugh. Those who know him well praise his integrity and honesty, and his dedication to improving himself and to helping

others. He has said that he can't stand people who make unkind comments behind other peoples' backs, and lives by the rule that you should never say something about someone that you wouldn't say to their face.

Christopher Alan Kirkpatrick was born on October 17, 1971 in Clarion, Pennsylvania. His father, Byron, died when Chris was very young, and his mother, Beverly, later remarried, giving Chris four half-sisters, Molly, Kate, Emily and Taylor. Clarion was a pleasant small town to grow up in, and Chris still feels proud to be a Pennsylvania native, supporting the Pittsburgh Steelers and Penn State Nittany Lions.

While Chris was still a kid, the family moved to Dayton, Ohio, where he soon made a whole new group of friends at school, playing a lot of sports and taking piano and singing lessons. With his family background, it was

perhaps inevitable that young Chris would take pleasure in a musical hobby: his grandmother was an opera singer, his grandfather recorded five country albums, and his mother is a voice teacher who also plays several instruments. Naturally talented and confident from an early age, Chris grew up singing in school, church and on the stage. As well as his musical talents and stage confidence, Chris was also academically gifted, and particularly excelled at languages. When high school came to an end, Chris saw no reason to leave full-time education – after all, he really enjoyed studying – and so enrolled at Valencia College in Dayton, initially majoring in the performing arts before transferring to psychology. His study of the mind taught him how music can affect people in many different ways, acting as therapy and touching the soul like nothing else. To pay the bills while in college, the ever-busy Chris put his voice, guitar and piano skills to good use by performing with local bands in coffee shops. Chris was also performing in theater productions around the Dayton area in his spare time, and remembers using his stage make-up to play a practical joke on his mother. For one show he had to

be made-up to look like an old man, so he decided to leave the make-up on when he returned home after the performance. He knocked on his mother's door and pretended to be the landlord, come to evict her for non-payment of the rent! Beverly wasn't taken in for a moment, but couldn't help laughing at her son's wicked sense of humor.

After two years at Valencia, the twenty-year-old Chris wanted a change of scene, and decided that it was time to follow his dream of working in the music industry. When his mother and stepfather had separated, Chris had remained close to his stepfather, who now lived in Orlando, Florida. Orlando was a perfect place to start a performing career: Universal Studios Florida, Disney and Nickelodeon were always on the lookout for talented youngsters for their stage and TV shows. So Chris moved to stay with his stepfather, enrolling on a part-time B.A. course at Rollins College, and working full-time at Universal Studios. It was while singing in a '50s-style doo-wop group called the Hollywood Hightones outside the diner at Universal, wearing period clothes and going by the nickname 'Spike', that Chris bumped into fellow performer Joey. Chris knew that what he really wanted to do was form a modern vocal group and try to make it in the cut-throat world of Top 40 pop, and he soon realized that Joey, along with JC and Justin (and eventually Lance), had the talent and dedication to help him achieve that dream.

Being a little older than the other guys, Chris had plenty of time to gain experience of life and romance before joining 'N Sync. He learnt early on that relationships are not always a bunch of roses: his first kiss came while playing kiss tag, but after the smooch the girl in question punched him and ran off. Chris jokes that this experience taught him early on that women are nothing but trouble!

During his time with 'N Sync, Chris has made no secret that he is on the lookout for a certain sort of girl – confident, intelligent and ambitious – and he finally seems to have found her. Former model Danielle Raabe first came into Chris's life while the band were making the video for 'I Drive Myself Crazy' – Danielle played his girlfriend – and the pair have been boyfriend and girlfriend in real life for the past eighteen months. Danielle now runs the business side of Chris's clothing and music production company FuManSkeeto, and often appears alongside Chris in interviews to promote the brand. Chris and Danielle make a perfect couple in interviews, always answering each other's questions and pretending to argue light-heartedly, and it is clear that they work as well together professionally as romantically. Chris has revealed that he knew Danielle was right for him soon after they met, when they just clicked personality-wise and decided that they had to work together. And if the other band members aren't around when Chris is feeling down, he knows he can turn to Danielle to give him a boost.

Chris has proved he is a creative force to be reckoned with

Although 'N Sync will always be his number one priority, FuManSkeeto has taken up a lot of Chris's time recently, and his work designing and marketing the clothes has given him another creative outlet outside the band. Chris originally came up with the

name while messing around with a friend in his hotel room while on tour: his story is that he saw a mosquito, which he nicknamed Fu Man Chu, which then became Fu Man Skeeto. Crazy, huh?

The clothing range, which is available from Nordstroms stores and through the Fu Man Skeeto website, includes sweaters, jersey shirts, tribal tattoo t-shirts and vintage Las Vegas hotel shirts. Chris has said that the philosophy behind the brand is to provide affordable, fashionable clothes which are accessible, sporty and casual, and are made from quality materials.

In an online interview, Chris and Danielle revealed that their ambitions for the brand include a range of children's clothes, which will be called Wigglers after a folk term for young mosquitoes. The company also plans to bring out a line of swimwear. As fans who attended 'N Sync's summer 2000 shows will know, FuManSkeeto has already branched out into music production, signing singer-songwriter Ron Irrizary, an old friend of Chris's from Dayton, Ohio. Chris and Ron both used to perform in local coffee shops while at college, and even used to write songs together. Chris has said that he feels that his own success should be shared with other equally talented individuals, and is glad to help promote people like Ron to a wider audience. Danielle added that FuManSkeeto's other ambitions include running summer camps, producing cartoons and action figures, and running a model search in order to put on catwalk shows.

In his spare time, of which there is never a great deal, Chris collects Bruce Lee memorabilia, swords, and anything related to The Beatles. Paul McCartney is one of Chris's all-time heroes, and he has admitted that he almost cried the day he met his idol in the flesh. Chris admires Michael Jackson as well, for reinventing pop music in the 1980s, and will join the rest of the band in inducting the King of Pop into the Rock'n'Roll Hall of Fame in June 2001.

Chris also has a reputation as an animal lover (perhaps that's why his clothing line is named after an insect!) and has two pet pug dogs named Busta and Korea. The pair have almost become honorary sixth and seventh members of the band: fans have set up websites devoted to the dogs, and until recently Busta used to travel with the band on tour, getting mobbed by fans almost as much as Chris himself!

When 'N Sync was formed, it was Chris who persuaded the other guys to give 100% effort at all times in order to make the band the success it is today. Now the ever-impatient, hardworking Chris has achieved a similar success with his side project, inspiring his FuManSkeeto team and working every waking hour to pursue his dream while still keeping 'N Sync on top of the world. With his unlimited energy and uncanny business sense, Chris has proved he is a creative force to be reckoned with. Whatever he turns his attention to next, you can be sure that this dedicated worker will put in as much effort as it takes to achieve his goals.

CHRIS FACTS

★ Chris is a regular bidder on Ebay.com, and recently bought Joey an original Superman arcade game

★ Chris's nicknames include Crazy, Psycho, Shorty and Pineapple

★ Chris has two tattoos - an 'N Sync logo flame on his ankle and a dragon on his calf

★ Chris got hold of a Playstation 2 from Japan months before they were released in the US, and became addicted to the Japanese games even though he couldn't understand the instructions!

★ Chris loves to watch baseball, and recently hung out at a Tampa vs. St. Louis game with Backstreet Boy Nick Carter

★ Chris loves Mexican food, especially tacos

★ Chris's first major purchase after the band became a success was a set of turntables

★ Chris really enjoyed visiting Japan – especially eating sushi!

★ Chris won a cookery competition at high school and ended up competing at the state finals!

★ Chris's dog Busta's favorite food is Butterfinger's candy

★ Chris's fave actress is Audrey Hepburn – he just loves the film *Breakfast at Tiffany's*

CHAPTER SEVEN

DIGITAL GETDOWN!

If you've ever attended an 'N Sync concert, whether it was one of their early support slots or a huge stadium show as part of their most recent *No Strings Attached* Tour, you'll know that these guys take performing very seriously. Lasers, pyrotechnics, elaborate sets and costume changes all add to the excitement and sense of occasion, but it's the five guys' synchronized choreography and close-harmony singing that is at the heart of every 'N Sync performance. They sure know how to put on a show!

The staging wasn't always so elaborate in the early days. When the group first started out supporting other acts and gaining experience, they didn't have the resources to work with a live band as they do today. The boys would perform their choreographed dance routines to a pre-recorded backing track, lip-syncing the words. Justin has admitted that the group

found this very frustrating – there was no scope to alter the pace of a track, or to be creative with the interpretation. In contrast, 'N Sync's most recent stadium shows featured a six-piece live band,

including two drummers, two keyboard players, a guitarist and a bass guitarist.

In the early years, the group developed a routine before each show to calm their nerves and loosen their bodies: they would play a game of hacky-sack, kicking a little bean bag around between them, keeping it in the air as long as possible. When 'N Sync toured with Janet Jackson in 1998, there just wasn't room backstage to play hacky-sack, so the guys made do with stretching exercises. Although dropping this element of their warm-up didn't seem to do any harm, they revived the tradition for their headlining tours in 1999 and 2000.

Another 'N Sync touring tradition is the group hug. Before every show, Justin, JC, Joey, Lance and Chris hook up with their stage crew, staff, and management – everyone backstage – for a prayer and a hug. JC has explained that 'N Sync see everyone who works with the band as their family, and this ritual ensures that the whole team is in sync before the show starts.

Over the years there have been a few moments when, despite all the luck and prayers, something has gone wrong with the show. Each member has his own stories of performance-related injuries: Chris remembers the moment he attempted a backflip on stage, but didn't quite manage it and landed on his head. The only thing damaged, luckily, was his pride! Once Joey landed badly after a particularly difficult dance move, spraining his ankle. He continued with the show in some pain, and when he removed his shoes after the show he discovered his toes had turned blue! And, of course, there's the time when Justin slipped on a wet stage in Germany in 1997 and broke his thumb. Despite being in considerable pain, this trooper managed to continue to the end of the performance, but he then had to wear a cast on his forearm for several weeks afterwards, which can be seen in some early photos of the band.

There have also been times when the guys haven't been too quick when it comes to working out where they are during a whistle-stop tour of foreign cities. In a live MSN chat, Justin admitted that the band regularly forget where they are performing, so they have to have the name of the city pasted on the dressing room door backstage. Joey admits that the worst moment came when the band was giving an interview in the tiny European country of Liechtenstein; he opened the interview with 'it's good to be here in Germany'!

When critics compare 'N Sync to that other musical phenomenon, Backstreet Boys, one point that is regularly made is the difference in their live shows. While Backstreet Boys shows have been conducted in the round with a glitzy, Hollywood feel, 'N Sync stick to an edgier, more personal staging which allows all five members to dance together and interact with the audience.

'N Sync's *No Strings Attached* tour, which kicked off in Biloxi, Mississippi on May 9, 2000 and ended in San Diego, California on December 2, 2000, was the longest and most ambitious live show the group has ever staged. It featured some of the most spectacular

Justin slipped on a wet stage in Germany in 1997 and broke his thumb

effects ever seen in a concert arena. Every night was sold out months in advance, but the show was also televised on HBO, allowing millions of fans across the country a front-row seat at the event of the year.

Hours before the fantastic five took to the stage, the audience was treated to performances from the specially selected pre-show acts. As well as short sets from sassy R&B singer Pink and former Dru Hill member Sisquo, the build-up also featured

singer-songwriter Ron Irizarry, who is managed by Chris's company Fu Man Skeeto Productions.

The main event would normally kick off around 9p.m., and as the house lights dimmed and the curtain rose, five figures could be seen hanging high above the stage. The crowd screamed as they realized that these were the 'N Sync boys, hanging on cables like unwanted marionettes. Just audible as the guys were slowly lowered to the stage was the theme music from Disney's *Pinocchio* – a smart touch.

In a symbolic move, Justin, JC, Joey, Lance and Chris pointedly tore off the velcro attaching the cables to their harnesses, and immediately launched into an explosive performance of *'No Strings Attached'* – complete with pyrotechnics so loud the fans could feel the detonations throughout the auditorium. Every move the guys made was accompanied by a wave of screams from the fired-up crowd.

The explosions continued through-out a funked-up version of 'I Want You Back', a completely new arrangement of this early hit single. To allow the guys a rest from the energetic opening routine, '(God Must Have Spent) A Little More Time on You' slowed the pace right down, giving Lance a chance to get his breath back while performing the spoken intro. For the final verse, the guys were raised high into the air on their own individual pedestals, as if they were still attached to cables. This part of the show didn't always go according to plan: during 'N Sync's appearance at the Erwin Center in Austin, Texas, Joey's pedestal failed to rise, and he was left waving at his four colleagues from ground level. Joey, ever the professional, played it cool and pretended nothing out of the ordinary had happened.

To allow the fivesome time to get down from the pedestals and change costumes, 'Tearin' Up My Heart' was introduced by an offbeat video clip featuring Ananda Lewis. The MTV VJ fronted a send-up of *Total Request Live*, asking the crowd to vote for which member of 'N Sync they'd like to be their personal slave for the day! After a storming performance of 'Tearin' Up My Heart', again with a new arrangement for the live show, Justin introduced 'It's Gonna Be Me' with a human beatbox performance which fans and reviewers alike judged to be pretty accomplished.

This highlight was followed by an 'N Sync concert fave: an uptempo version of 'I Drive Myself Crazy' performed on a set that recreated a typical suburban living room. In his spoken intro, Chris said that he would have liked to invite the whole crowd to their living room in Orlando, but because the crowd was too big they'd decided to bring their living room to the arena!

A memorable rendition of 'I Thought She Knew' was followed by a wacky video clip showing Lance being questioned by Regis Philbin on the set of *Who Wants to be a Millionaire*. In the clip, Lance wins the million and is showered by confetti, triggering a storm of the stuff which was blown across the stage and into the crowd during the next song, 'Just Got Paid'.

After a short break, the guys returned to the stage rising through the floor on hydraulic lifts, performing a futuristic Western routine for 'Space Cowboy (Yippie-Yi-Yay)' before disappearing back into the floor. For 'It Makes Me Ill' the boys drew literal inspiration from the song, wearing doctor's coats and feigning sickness at the end of an energetic and inspiring dance routine.

Another highlight for many fans was 'N Sync's performance of 'This I Promise You'. The group performed this song on a section of the stage that slowly moved through the arena, right up to the very back, allowing every fan to get a close-up view of their fave 'N Syncer. Using the hydraulic platform, the boys were able to get close-up with their fans, throwing their towels into the crowd and shaking hands with those nearest to them.

It was all change again for the next track, 'Digital Getdown', a sci-fi extravaganza worthy of a Hollywood blockbuster movie. Wearing glow-in-the-dark costumes, the guys entered through slits in a huge screen, and the low lighting meant their clothes lit up as they went through their complex dance moves. Performing on moving walkways at the sides of the stage, the guys handed out glow-in-the-dark gifts to lucky fans.

After all that had gone before, 'N Sync's spectacular performance of 'Bye Bye Bye' was made even more poignant by the fact that it was the last song. The boys entered wearing monk's robes and intoning a medieval chant, before launching into a frenzied routine which proved that their energy had not been drained by the previous ninety minutes' performance.

In an interview before the group's show in Foxboro, near Boston, Massachusetts, Chris emphasized how tired the guys feel after the show, expressing the hope that fans would be as exhausted as the group as they left the arena. He added that if the guys aren't physically and emotionally drained when they walk onto their tour bus, they don't feel they've given a good show.

Wearing glow-in-the-dark costumes, the guys entered through slits in a huge screen

'N Sync weren't too tired, however, to help out their old friend Britney by appearing in a video clip during

her summer 2000 shows. Justin, JC, Joey, Lance and Chris introduced themselves to Britney's fans (as if they didn't know who they were!) and invited

Throughout the summer 2000 shows, Justin kept his trademark curls under wraps, wearing a succession of bandanas and beanie hats to hide his new hairstyle

audience members to enter a competition to meet Britney on stage. It was a fun way to give something back to Britney in return for her performance as one of the opening acts on 'N Sync's first headlining tour. Throughout the summer 2000 shows, Justin kept his

trademark curls under wraps, wearing a succession of bandanas and beanie hats to hide his new hairstyle. Sharp-eyed fans eventually spotted the transformation; Justin's hair had been tightly braided and woven into patterns, in a style similar to that of Latrell Sprewell of the New York Knicks.

Justin's new style only lasted for a few weeks before it was back to curls, but it was only one of a number of surprises that 'N Sync unveiled in 2000. What 'N Sync will have in store on the summer 2001 tour is anyone's guess right now, but you can be sure that they are already planning a few surprises to take the 'N Sync live experience to the next level. We can't wait!

CHAPTER EIGHT

JOEY UP CLOSE

When they're feeling down and in need of a laugh and a chat, who do the other members of 'N Sync turn to for light relief? Joey Fatone, of course. This easy-going joker with a great sense of fun doesn't take life too seriously, and can be relied on to make light of any situation. Whether it's his outrageous dress

This tall, dark and handsome chap is never happier than when surrounded by beautiful females

sense, quickfire quotes from comedy shows like *South Park* or his high-speed New York banter, there's something about Joey that instantly puts people at ease.

It's perhaps due to his easy-going nature and natural chattiness that Joey is such an incredible flirt! This tall, dark and handsome chap is never happier than when surrounded by beautiful females, and he has developed quite a reputation as the 'ladies man' of the group. Joey admits that he loves the company of women – and when there are thousands screaming his name at an 'N Sync show, he's in his element!

Joey was born Joseph Anthony Fatone Jr. on January 28, 1977 in Brooklyn, New York. His parents, Joe and

Phyllis, already had two young children, Janine and Steven, who were five and two years old respectively when Joey arrived. Part of a tight-knit local community, the Fatones were regular churchgoers who took part in community theater and music shows. Joe was a central figure in the life of the neighborhood, and sung as part of a locally famous doo-wop group, the Orions, who performed music by artists such as the Temptations and Frankie Lymon and the Teenagers.

Growing up surrounded by music from the 1950s and 1960s, as well as that of modern vocal R&B acts like Boyz II Men, young Joey loved to sing around the house. One of his earliest memories is working out a whole song and dance routine for the song 'Tequila', a performance which gained him a round of applause from anyone lucky enough to witness it.

When Joey was around thirteen years old, the family began to feel that inner-city Brooklyn wasn't the best place to bring up their teenagers, and after a lot of thought the family decided to relocate to Orlando, Florida, where the weather was better, as were the house prices and schools. Joey settled in well and attended Dr. Phillips High School, where he began to take an interest in school musicals and concerts.

singing for the tourists at Universal Studios, he realized he wasn't ever going to get noticed by a talent scout while hidden under layers of monster make-up! As every 'N Sync fan knows, Joey's next move was to hook up with JC, his buddy Justin, and Chris, who was also performing at Universal Studios, to form a vocal group which would eventually make history.

Ask any Joey fan what would be the perfect gift for their main man, and the answer would be immediate:

Joey enjoyed acting the fool and singing for the tourists at Universal Studios

anything to do with Superman! This supercool guy is a passionate collector of memorabilia related to the man of steel, and has a whole room at his parents' house devoted to storing his collection. The obsession started when he was just eight years old. Little Joey would tie a cape round his shoulders and run around pretending to fly – and once jumped from a second-floor window to prove that he really could soar like Superman! Luckily the little guy had thought to put a thin mattress below the window to break his fall, but the escapade still ended in a trip to the emergency room for stitches!

Although all the guys love signing autographs and meeting their fans, Joey is the one who's always happy to spend an extra few minutes chatting to fans outside the auditorium, even when the band are running late and need to get to the soundcheck. Joey just hates to say no! Never one to pass up the opportunity to mingle with beautiful ladies, Joey was lucky enough to be a presenter at the Miss Teen USA

pageant in 1998, where he has joked that he handed out his phone number to all 51 contestants, without any success!

He might be pretty confident these days, but it could all have turned out very differently. The first time Joey took a girl to the cinema, at the age of thirteen, he bought her a drink and some popcorn, but she dumped him straight away – poor Joey! Joey has always been confident with fellow performers, and recalls that he was always the band member to

introduce himself and the other guys to celebrities when the band was first starting out. When 'N Sync toured Europe in 1997, they became firm friends with Scandinavian pop group Aqua, most famous for

'N SYNC
← FOLD OUT FOR MORE PHOTOS

Opposite page: Joey with Leann Rimes

of the spotlight to avoid upsetting Joey's young female fans.

However, as the band returned to the States to pick up their career on home turf, and Aqua became bigger in Europe than they were in the USA, mature and sensible Joey realized that the couple could not be girlfriend and boyfriend any longer. Pop stars' lives are ruled by immovable schedules, and the pair would never have been able to spend time together, so Joey and Lene agreed to go their separate ways.

Joey admits that 'N Sync's busy schedule doesn't make it easy to build a lasting relationship. He has been linked with several young women, including *Clueless* actress Elisa Donovon, who also appeared in the 'I Drive Myself Crazy' video and Danay from girl band Innosense. The closest Joey has to a girlfriend is an old friend from Orlando, named Kelly, who he sees whenever he goes home. It's clear that Joey has a lot of affection for Kelly, bringing her to awards ceremonies and wearing a friendship ring she once gave him, but he has made it clear that this isn't a serious romantic relationship.

'Barbie Girl', who often appeared on the same bill at concerts and TV shows. Joey got on particularly well with the group's beautiful Norwegian singer Lene Nystrom, and romance blossomed as they hung out together after shows.

Surprisingly, it was Lene who did the running to start with, according to Joey, who was more used to having to woo a prospective date with smooth talk. Fellow pop star Lene was a good match for Joey in many ways, because she understood the pressure he was under, and was keen to keep their relationship out

Joey admits that 'N Sync's busy schedule doesn't make it easy to build a lasting relationship

This energetic and positive guy might not yet have found Ms. Right, but he's having a lot of fun looking as he performs all over the world. He's also a superhero to many, many 'N Sync fans; with his music, dancing, acting and producing super-powers, who knows what he'll turn to next?

JOEY FACTS

★ If a movie was made about 'N Sync, Joey would like to be played by David Schwimmer (Ross from *Friends*)

★ Joey's all-time fave movie is *Willy Wonka and the Chocolate Factory*

★ Joey's fave food is Italian; he's never happier than when sitting down to a big bowl of pasta

★ If Joey could relive one day of his life, it would be the day he graduated from high school

★ His number one book is *Macbeth* by William Shakespeare

★ Joey wishes his feet were a size smaller

★ Joey's nicknames include Phat-One, Superman and Party Animal

★ Joey loves to travel, and particularly enjoys visiting London, South Africa and South East Asia

★ He once received a hand-knitted Superman sweater from a fan, but he's afraid to wear it in case he damages it!

★ Joey has been voted the most talkative member of 'N Sync by the other guys

★ His worst habits are biting his nails and laziness

★ CHAPTER NINE
FIVE COOL GUYS!

For Justin, JC, Joey, Chris and Lance, being a member of 'N Sync is definitely the most important thing in their lives. But despite putting 100% effort into the group's tours, music and promotion, every one of the band members has also found time to pursue his own solo projects outside of 'N Sync, giving each guy the opportunity to follow his dreams and ambitions in other fields.

Lance is without doubt the most entrepreneurial and business-minded member of 'N Sync, and has been involved in the business and planning side of the group since the guys first got together. He has always been a big fan of country music, and has helped the other band members to appreciate the talents of various country artists over the years, playing their music on the tour bus or backstage. Combining his passions for business and music, in 1998 Lance set up a management company, cleverly named FreeLance Entertainment, specializing in country artists. The company, which now employs Lance's mother and sister, conducted a countrywide talent search in association with MTV, and drew an incredible response, uncovering some truly talented artists.

Their first signing was Meredith Edwards, a teenage country singer who supported 'N Sync on some tour dates in 1999.

In December 2000 Edwards released her first single, 'A Rose is a Rose', followed by her debut album *Reach* in March 2001. After Lance attended six open auditions across the US during 'N Sync's *No Strings Attached* Tour, FreeLance also signed Jack DeFeo, a New-York born singer who was discovered while peforming as Hercules at Universal Studios' Wild Wild West stunt show.

Lance's talent for organisation and management also came in handy when FreeLance Entertaiment threw a huge New Year's bash at the end of 2000. In association with MTV, the $200-a-ticket *Millennium New Year's Eve Jam 2001* was held at New York City's Roseland Ballroom. Guests included JC, Joey and Justin, while those performing included Nelly, Ludacris, Black Rob and the Sugar Hill Gang. The star-studded event was judged to be a great success,

JC has proved that he is happiest in the recording studio, collaborating with artists in diverse musical genres

thanks to Lance's steady hand behind the scenes. It's not just Lance who has been bitten by the music bug – JC has proved that he is happiest in the recording studio, collaborating with artists in diverse

musical genres. After his successful writing debut for girl group Wild Orchid, dark horse JC has been helping out with the career of another young act, Boyz'n'Girls United, by writing and producing a song entitled 'Messed Around' for their debut self-titled album. The group appeared as a support act on 'N Sync's *No Strings Attached* Tour, and look set for greater things in the future. JC also recently appeared on the new album by R&B act Blaque, performing on a track entitled 'Bring It All to Me', and guested on jazz saxophonist Steve Grove's project Euge Groove, performing the song 'Give In To Me'.

In a move that shows Justin has a mature head on his young shoulders, this generous guy has stepped up his involvement with the Giving Back Fund, an organisation which helps channel donations from celebrities into community projects across the country. Justin has also established the Justin Timberlake Foundation, a non-profit organisation which funds music and arts projects in public schools.

Justin also gave up some of his time and energy for a good cause in January 2001, when he appeared alongside other celebrities, including Ethan Hawke and Uma Thurman, in a *Marie Claire* campaign to promote gun law reform. Wearing a T-shirt bearing the slogan 'End Gun Violence Now' and holding hands with a lucky girl named Gillan Nadel, Justin was quoted as saying 'When the constitution was drafted, AK-47s didn't exist. Now, at the very least, people should support safety locks for guns.'

Justin has also taken the opportunity to work with some of the music world's biggest stars, artists that he admires and who have become close friends. He has always been a huge fan of Brian McKnight, and he has admitted that it was a privilege to be invited to duet with McKnight on his new album, released in the spring of 2001. Although McKnight is keeping the album title under wraps for now, it's been revealed that the collaboration is titled 'My Kind of Girl'. Another of Justin's heroes, Stevie Wonder, also guests on the record. For his part, Brian has said that Justin was great to work with – refreshingly free of arrogance, always willing to learn and very talented – and that he believes 'N Sync will be around for a very long time to come.

Joey remains committed to his dream of developing an acting career in parallel with his work with 'N Sync

Showing that Justin's tastes cross musical boundaries, he has also recorded a duet with R&B star Usher, in which the desirable pair 'battle' over a girl along the lines of Brandy and Monica's hit 'The Boy is Mine'.

Chris continues to pour his creative energy into Fu Man Skeeto's range of clothing and accessories – check out their website, www.fumanskeeto.com – and recently turned his hand to artist management with Fu Man Skeeto's signing of Ron Arrizary, a talented singer-songwriter who supported 'N Sync on their *No Strings Attached* Tour. Another activity which keeps Chris busy is his role as spokesperson for Child Watch, a charity-funded program which aims to safeguard children from kidnapping and raise awareness of the risk of abduction.

Joey remains committed to his dream of developing an acting career in parallel with his work with 'N Sync, and Joey fans are already anticipating his feature debut in a movie entitled *My Big Fat Greek Wedding*. He has also been offered two different lead parts alongside Lance in his forthcoming movie project *On The L*, but reportedly hasn't decided which one to take yet. Other movie plans are in the works, as Joey gets involved in the business behind the scenes, promoting and financing new films by up-and-coming directors.

Despite their busy schedule and solo projects, 'N Sync are always willing to devote their time and energy to charity events and to promote causes that are close to their hearts. 'N Sync's annual Challenge for the Children basketball game, an all-celebrity match which benefits various childrens' charities, raised over $500,000 in August 2000. As an example of the way in which the money is used, 'N Sync donated $15,000 to Childplace, a shelter for abused and neglected children in Jeffersonville, Indiana. The shelter's director, Nathan Samual, who received

Justin, JC, Joey, Lance and Chris have always been keen to show that they are not just another pop group

the donation out of the blue, was quoted as saying, 'Usually our kids are the ones that don't get the nice stuff, and have been put though the tough circumstances in life. Now they're the ones others envy. Their heads are so big – they hardly believe it, really.' The next Challenge for the Children game is planned for Las Vegas in early July 2001.

The guys are also keen to use their status as role models in a responsible way, and during the half-time ad break in 2001's Superbowl XXXV, a new Anheuser-Busch commercial aired featuring the five 'N Syncers thanking parents for talking to their children about underage drinking. 'N Sync have done their bit for the environment as well, helping to protect the world's endangered tiger population by adopting a wild tiger as part of the Stars In the Wild scheme.

Justin, JC, Joey, Lance and Chris have always been keen to show that they are not just another pop group, and their various projects and interests, both individually and as a group, prove that these are five intelligent young men with good hearts and creative minds. Who knows what will emerge next from the fertile imaginations of the five?

CHAPTER TEN

LANCE UP CLOSE

Blond, green-eyed cutie Lance Bass comes across as courteous and polite in interviews, always careful with his words and happy to tell the world about life with 'N Sync. But surely there must be another side to Lance, a different aspect of his personality that he hides from the public? Not a chance! With Lance, what you see is what you get. Both on and off stage, hanging out with the guys or working with producers in the studio, Lance is renowned for his gentlemanly manner and businesslike attitude to life. His fellow band members admire the way he remains calm and relaxed in any situation, and he can be relied on to see the bigger picture whenever there's a disagreement.

James Lance Bass was born on May 4, 1979 in Clinton, Mississippi, a rural town a long way from any of the state's large cities. His parents, Jim and Diane Bass, welcomed a little brother for three-year-old Stacy, and the Bass children had a pretty idyllic upbringing, playing in the fields and attending church regularly. Lance enjoyed singing in the choir, and as he moved through school his interest in music grew. As he entered his mid-teens, Lance's voice broke, becoming deeper and stronger, and he soon realized that he was now a perfect fit for the bass part in a choir, singing the deepest notes. He started

taking singing lessons with a voice coach to improve his breathing and technique.

Outside of school and church he joined a show choir, Attaché, who took part in competitions and concerts up and down the country. It was Lance's first taste of touring with a band, and he loved both the sense of freedom and the opportunity to see more of the USA.

Lance played baseball, football and basketball at school, although he would be the first to admit that he's not a born sportsman or even particularly co-ordinated. He has revealed that he found it hard to pick up the complex dance routines when he first started in the group, and often finds himself the butt of the other guys' jokes whenever he joins them on the basketball court for a few hoops.

As well as playing sports, Lance got good grades in his studies at high school, and was Vice President of his class. Although he says he only joined them to get out of other classes, Lance was also a member of several school clubs including Student Council, Students against Drunk Driving, FCA, Fellowship of Christian Athletes, Honor Society, Youth In Government and the Mayor's Youth Council.

This smart and ambitious young kid who continually got good grades was always going to aim high when it came to a career, and Lance's parents were

pleased when he set his sights on working for NASA and perhaps becoming an astronaut. Lance has revealed that the seed of this dream was planted when he spent a week on Space Camp at the Kennedy Space Center when he was in seventh grade. Even now, having circled the world with 'N Sync and achieved more than many people ever dream of, he would still give anything for a ride in the Space Shuttle!

As well as playing sports, Lance got good grades in his studies at high school, and was Vice President of his class

Lance was sent pretty sky-high by an incredible gift sent to him by a dedicated fan during the group's 1999 tour. She had put together a photo album containing photographs of the Apollo space missions signed by all the astronauts, including Buzz Aldrin and Neil Armstrong. It had been in her family since the 1960s and Lance will treasure it forever.

Unlike the other members of 'N Sync, while Lance was growing up he didn't hold a particularly strong desire to make it big in the show business world. He was a dedicated singer, but before he met the rest of the guys he was happy just performing at talent shows and local church concerts. In the summer of 1995, when Lance was just sixteen, he received a call from a guy named Justin, inviting him to come down to Florida because his band was looking for a fifth member. At first Lance didn't believe the call was genuine – he had his high school homecoming next day and was more interested in that. His old vocal coach, who was put on the line to persuade him that

the offer was serious, had recommended Lance to the guys down in Orlando.

Lance's mom, Diane, a sixth-grade teacher, took some persuading to let her son take off for sunny Florida to meet some guys he hardly knew, but Lance eventually managed to win her over. Lance has said that he knew the band was going to be huge as soon as he met Justin, JC, Joey and Chris. They bonded immediately; the other guys realized Lance was the missing piece of the jigsaw, and by the end of the day he was in the band.

Lance is still very close to his mother, who accompanied the band as a chaperone during their first tour of Europe. For her part, Diane is devoted to her son, and has collected over 20 scrapbooks of 'N Sync photographs and memorabilia since the band started. Lance has revealed that she is also proud to give away 'N Sync goodies to the kids who get the best grades in her class.

Lance has said that he knew the band was going to be huge as soon as he met Justin, JC, Joey and Chris

In an online Yahoo chat with mother and son, Diane was asked to describe Lance in ten words or less, and her reaction sums up the appeal of Lance to us all: 'Good lookin', sweet, friendly, the best son in the whole wide world.' Awww!

Now that 'N Sync has given Lance the financial freedom to pursue his dreams, this homebody has made building the perfect home his first priority. The property has a large swimming pool and a tropical garden in which Lance can chill out and play with his beloved dogs.

Another of Lance's passions is for country music; he has been a huge fan of Garth Brooks since his early teenage years, and was thrilled to meet him at the CMA awards in 1999. He counts the Dixie Chicks and Alabama among his fave artists, and he has admitted that 'N Sync's collaboration with Alabama on the track '(God Must Have Spent) A Little More Time on You' was a dream come true.

When it comes to romance, Lance has said that he would like to find someone who shares his faith

This religious guy's number one book to read is the bible, and along with the rest of the group he is proud to wear his WWJD (What Would Jesus Do?) bracelet. When it comes to romance, Lance has said that he would like to find someone who shares his faith, and with whom he could be best friends for a while before getting serious. He has said that he also looks for innocence, good morals and an honest approach to life – oh, and a pair of beautiful eyes. Right now Lance is still looking for the right girl, and has so much going on in his life that he just isn't able to give anyone his undivided attention.

As to whether he'd ever date a fan, Lance has never said no, and has modestly admitted that he has met some fans who were so attractive that he was rendered speechless with embarrassment. It just goes to show that not all pop stars are super-confident and comfortable with the adoration stardom brings. Technology-friendly Lance has been bitten by the Internet bug, and spends hours surfing the net when he gets the chance. He often checks out 'N Sync-related sites, and has admitted to going online to chat on 'N Sync bulletin boards under the name 'IMPOOFU'. Look out for him next time you're online! Check out FreelanceEnt.com, too – this is Lance's management company, in which Lance takes a leading hand, assisted by his mother Diane and sister Stacey, the company's first two employees.

If there's one thing that Lance likes about being in 'N Sync more than anything else, it's the opportunity to travel the world visiting foreign countries and meeting new people. Lance collects antique knives, and during 'N Sync's travels he was particularly taken by his experiences in Asia, where he found some fascinating items to add to his collection. However, one place that Lance won't be going back to in a hurry is Cancun in Mexico. He was tricked into taking part in a bullfight, which turned out to be a terrifying and painful experience that he has no wish to repeat!

If there's one thing that Lance likes about being in 'N Sync more than anything else, it's the opportunity to travel the world

For many fans, Lance is the perfect guy: sensitive, intelligent, spiritual and charming in equal measure. It's these qualities that enable him to fit in so well in the 'N Sync gang, despite being the last member to join. No doubt all the other guys would agree that 'N Sync wouldn't be 'N Sync without him.

LANCE FACTS

★ Lance's fave ice cream is toffee pecan

★ Lance's nicknames include Scoop and Stealth

★ Lance admits his worst habit is biting his bottom lip

★ If he had to take one movie to a desert island it would be *Clue*, because he loves the dialogue

★ If Lance could drive any car it would be a Lamborghini

★ Lance's fave TV show of all time is *I Love Lucy*, and his number one actress is Lucille Ball

★ For breakfast he loves to eat French toast

★ Lance used to support the Orlando Magic NBA team, but now supports the Los Angeles Lakers because LA is his second home

★ He is a big fan of watersports, especially jet-skiing and scuba diving

★ Lance spent his first big paycheck on a new car

★ Lance dyed his hair blue for a couple of days, but he didn't like it much so he quickly bleached it back to normal

★ Lance's acting hero is Tom Hanks

★ Of all the places he has visited, Lance most enjoyed Liechtenstein

★ CHAPTER ELEVEN
'N THE FUTURE

So what does a band whose last album sold over a million copies in one day do for an encore? What could the guys who have everything possibly want next? In 'N Sync's case, the plan is to ensure that the next album gives their fans even more of what makes 'N Sync special – to make a record that's even better than the superlative *No Strings Attached*.

The guys are aware that making the fastest-selling record of all time is a hard act to follow, but they've said that they don't feel any pressure to match their own record of 2.4 million copies sold in one week. They've given themselves plenty of time to relax in the studio and get a vibe going, and there's a positive atmosphere in the 'N Sync camp about the new record. JC has said that the fact that 2001 is a whole new year and whole new millennium has inspired them to start from scratch, building a fresh sound without looking back at what has come before.

Justin has revealed that the new album, as yet untitled, will have even more energy than *No Strings Attached*, with a more stylized feel. In a press conference to announce the nominations for the 43rd Annual Grammy Awards, JC revealed more about the philosophy behind the new album. The 'aggressive' pop sound that the group first introduced to the world with 'I

Want You Back' has now swept the music world, with many other pop acts using similar sounds and working with the same producers. Now 'N Sync feel it's time for a change. 'I think it's time to find something a little funky,' said JC. 'We're going to experiment with sounds and try to create something new.'

The group started out in a Florida studio in early 2001 crafting their own sound on a number of tracks, before enlisting the help some of the world's leading R&B and hip-hop producers to work on specific songs. Justin hinted that the band might again work with Kevin 'She'kspere' Briggs, who produced 'It Makes Me Ill' on *No Strings Attached* and has also worked with Pink and Mariah Carey. Richard Marx, the 1980s pop star who wrote and produced the band's smash hit ballad 'This I Promise You' is also expected to work on some tracks on the new album.

As was the case during the making of *No Strings Attached*, the guys will record far more tracks than are needed. This approach allows them to choose only the strongest, to create a truly cohesive album that showcases only their best songs.

There have also been suggestions that the group will collaborate on a track with the country singer Jo Dee

Messina. That is something which would be sure to please country-loving Lance, as would suggestions that the group may record a special country version of 'This I Promise You' at some point in the future.

To summarize his view of the way the new songs

Since early 1999, Justin, JC, Joey, Lance and Chris have talked in interviews about making a film based on their experiences in the music industry

were shaping up, Justin said, 'We're just taking this dirty pop vibe to the next level.' He also hinted that the new single, which looks set to be released in late spring 2001, will have a more eclectic feel than 'N Sync's previous hits. And in a move which shows the band evolving personally and musically, each

member will have some writing credits on the album, either by the inclusion of self-penned songs or collaborations with other writers.

The new album is slated for release in the early summer, but no firm date has been set. The CD is eagerly anticipated by fans and music industry insiders alike, but 'N Sync aren't prepared to rush things; as Chris said in an MTV interview, 'We're not going to do anything else until we get it right.'

Despite the fact that the music is still evolving, the guys have already announced another major summer stadium tour around the release of the CD, with the first date at Miami's Pro Player Stadium on May 12, 2001. With a mammoth tour on the cards and a surefire blockbuster CD virtually in the can, 2001 looks set to be remembered for the Summer of

'N Sync. However, it might be a case of 'enjoy it while you can', because it's been suggested that after this tour the guys plan to take a break from band activities for a while to focus on their solo projects.

'N Sync fans should have no cause for despair, however, because there will be another treat on the horizon to tempt 'N Sync fans soon: the group's long-awaited movie! Following their ill-fated appearance in the straight-to-video *Jack Of All Trades* alongside Britney Spears and Kenny Rogers, the guys are now looking to the future.

Since early 1999, Justin, JC, Joey, Lance and Chris have talked in interviews about making a film based on their experiences in the music industry. After long discussions with various production companies and film studios, the group have signed up with the Total Film Group, a small and relatively new company which has not produced a large number of movies in the past. From the outset the guys have insisted on a great deal of artistic control, and felt that this could be best achieved by working with a small company whose staff were willing to put their hearts and souls into the project.

'N Sync will always be five guys who have been friends from day one

Despite suggestions that the film would bear some similarities to the Spice Girls' movie *Spiceworld*, the band have insisted that they won't be playing themselves. Instead they have revealed that they will be playing fictional characters in a story with a musical slant, and will also be involved in scripting the movie and orchestrating its launch. Lance, for one, has been quick to counter the *Spiceworld* comparisons, joking that their movie would be much better because 'we actually have a budget for this one!'

The guys have already visited Universal Studios Florida to film a teaser ad for the as-yet-untitled movie, which features the band arriving at the movie's premiere at the Cannes Film Festival, and the release date looks likely to be sometime in the late summer of 2001.

The ever-busy Lance has also been making his individual mark in the world of film production. In early 2001 he teamed up with a former exec at Tom Hanks' organization to found his own production company, named 'A Happy Place', which aims to create soundtrack-driven feature vehicles for musicians and athletes. The first film to be made will star Lance and fellow 'N Syncer Joey, and will be titled *On The L*. With a budget of a cool $10m, the movie tells the story of a couple who meet briefly on Chicago's subway system, but are separated and must find a way to get back together. The film is to be distributed by Miramax, and production began in March 2001. The big question for 'N Sync fans is: who will play the lead female role? Although America's hottest young actresses must be lining up to star opposite the blond cutie, no details have been released as yet.

Justin also looks likely to branch out into more acting roles in the future. He admits he has been reading a few film scripts, but isn't ready to take a leading role right now due to his commitments with the band. We may just see Mr Timberlake tipped for the Best Supporting Actor role at the Academy Awards very soon!

So what else can we expect to see from this talented bunch of guys in the longer term? During the group's *Larry King Live* interview, Chris made the point that all the guys consider themselves to be very business-minded and aware of what they can achieve now they are financially secure. They are keen to get involved in nurturing and promoting new acts, using the knowledge they have picked up to help others get started in show business. Along with the others, Chris expressed the wish to get more involved in writing and producing behind the scenes in the future.

Although they never sound cynical or jaded, all of the guys became aware of the pitfalls of success at a very young age, and have learnt from this experience. They have said that their ambition as a group is now to emulate artists such as Madonna and George Michael, whose sound and image evolved with their fans while still gaining critical acclaim and commercial success.

However 'N Sync's music changes and evolves, and whatever outside projects its members get involved in, 'N Sync will always be five guys who have been friends from day one. So whenever interviewers ask whether 'N Sync will stay together, the answer is always the same: of course! After all, even if they weren't famous, these guys would still be calling each other up to write together, because at the end of the day they're just a bunch of talented young men who love making music.

A-Z OF 'N Sync

A is for Alabama, the country rock group who re-recorded '(God Must Have Spent) A Little More Time On You' with backing vocals by 'N Sync

B is for Busta, Chris's pug dog and an honorary sixth member of the band

C is for ceiling fan, the strangest thing the guys have ever had to sign, and also for Chris, the craziest member of 'N Sync

D is for Disney; not only did the *Mickey Mouse Club* give JC and Justin their big break, but the group's first ever live show was at Walt Disney World in Florida.

E is for entertainment, what every 'N Sync show is all about

F is for faith, something that is very important to every member of 'N Sync

G is for green: JC would love to dye his hair the colour of astroturf if he had the guts!

H is for hackey-sack, which the guys play before every show

I is for 'I Want You Back', 'N Sync's first US single.

J is for Joey, Justin and JC, of course!

K is for knishes, a snack the guys love to sample when they visit New York City

L is for Lance, the charming southern gentleman with the deep Bass voice

M is for the *Mickey Mouse Club*, the TV show which brought JC and Justin together

N is for *No Strings Attached*, the group's Diamond-selling masterpiece album

O is for Orlando, the sunny Florida city where the band was born

P is for Platinum, the rating every 'N Sync album has achieved many times over

Q is for quick-change – during an 'N Sync show the guys have to slip into several different costumes in superfast time!

R is for romance, something the guys don't find much time for in their crazy schedule

S is for Superman, Joey's all-time hero!

T is for tattoos, which can be found on every guy's ankle except JC's – he's terrified of needles.

U is for Uri Geller, the British psychic who advised the band to use a star on their first album for luck – it worked!

V is for video games – all the guys love to play computer games in their spare time, especially driving games and sports simulations

X is for Xmas, every 'N Sync member's fave time of year

Y is for you, the fans who have made 'N Sync the success they are today.

Z is for ZZZ, JC's favorite pastime!

'N SYNC

← **FOLD OUT FOR MORE PHOTOS**

'N Sync
ALBUM DISCOGRAPHY AND VIDEOGRAPHY

ALBUMS

'N Sync (European release)
May 1997
Tearin' Up My Heart
You Got It
Sailing
Crazy For You
Riddle
For the Girl Who Has Everything
Giddy Up
Here We Go
Best Of My Life
More Than a Feeling
I Want You Back
Together Again
Forever Young

'N Sync (US release)
April 1998
Tearin' Up My Heart
I Just Wanna Be With You
Here We Go
For the Girl Who Has Everything
(God Must Have Spent) A Little More Time
On You
You Got It
I Need Love
I Want You Back
Everything I Own
I Drive Myself Crazy
Crazy For You
Sailing
Giddy Up

Home For Christmas
November 1998
Home For Christmas
Under My Tree
I Never Knew The Meaning of Christmas
Merry Christmas, Happy Holidays
The Christmas Song
(Chestnuts Roasting On an Open Fire)
I Guess It's Christmas Time
All I Want is You This Christmas
The First Noel
In Love On Christmas
It's Christmas
O Holy Night (A Capella)
Love's In Our Hearts On Christmas Day
The Only Gift
Kiss Me At Midnight

No Strings Attached
March 2001
Bye Bye Bye
It's Gonna Be Me
Space Cowboy (Yippie-Yi-Yay)
Just Got Paid
It Makes Me Ill
This I Promise You
No Strings Attached
Digital Get Down
Bringin' Da Noise
That's When I'll Stop Loving You
I'll Be Good For You
I Thought She Knew

VIDEOS

'N Sync: 'N The Mix
November 1998
I Want You Back
Tearin' Up My Heart
For The Girl Who Has Everything
Here We Go
(God Must Have Spent)
A Little More Time On You
Merry Christmas, Happy Holidays

'N Sync:
Live From Madison Square Garden
December 2000
No Strings Attached
I Want You Back
(God Must Have Spent)
A Little More Time On You
Tearin' Up My Heart
Justin's Beat Box
It's Gonna Be Me
I Drive Myself Crazy
I Thought She Knew
Just Got Paid
Space Cowboy (Yippie-Yi-Yay)
It Makes Me Ill
This I Promise You
Digital Get Down
Bye Bye Bye

'N Sync Making the Tour
December 2000

WEBSITES
Check out these websites for the latest news and information on 'N Sync:

www.nsync.com
www.nsyncfansunited.com
www.nsyncstudio.com
www.always-nsync.com

www.musicfans.to/nsyncover21
www.nsyncworld.com
www.nsyncdirect.com
www.abstracts.net/justin-timberlake-nsync/